# Wild Animal Kingdom

# RABBITS

## GAIL TERP

**BLACK RABBIT BOOKS**

Bolt is published by Black Rabbit Books
P.O. Box 3263, Mankato, Minnesota, 56002.
www.blackrabbitbooks.com
Copyright © 2017 Black Rabbit Books

Design and Production by Michael Sellner
Photo Research by Rhonda Milbrett

Library of Congress Control Number: 2015954912

HC ISBN: 978-1-68072-056-3    PB ISBN: 978-1-68072-313-7

Printed in the United States at CG Book Printers,
North Mankato, Minnesota, 56003. PO #1798 4/16

Web addresses included in this book were working and appropriate at the time of publication. The publisher is not responsible for broken or changed links.

## Image Credits
Adobe Stock: nmelnychuk, 11 (top);
Corbis: SHAMIL ZHUMATOV, 26–27;
Dreamstime: Twildlife, 3; Getty: John Dominis,
15 (bottom); istock: Bernhard Richter, 22; Me–
che, 24; saje, 25; stanley45, 17; Zippher29, 23 (top);
Nat Geo: HEIDI & HANS–JUERGEN KOCH/ MINDEN
PICTURES, 12; RICH REID, 11 (bottom); Photoshot: Andia/
Photoshot, 14 (top); Science Source: G. Ronald Austing, 8;
Shutterstock: ariman, 18, 19 (silhouette); cellistka, 29 (snake);
Cipariss, 29 (bark); Claudia Paulussen, Cover; Darrell Blake
Courtney, Back Cover, 1; Eric Isselee, 15 (top); Evlakhov Valeriy,
29 (wolf); Jim Larkin, 23 (bottom); Kuttelvaserova Stuchelova,
31; Lincoln Rogers, 4–5; oksana2010, 29 (rabbit); photomas-
ter, 29 (owl); Pressmaster, 32; scattoselvaggio, 14 (bottom);
Scisetti Alfio, 29 (clover); Simun Ascic, 20–21; Victoria
Novak, 18 (background); Zhukov Oleg, 6–7
Every effort has been made to contact copyright
holders for material reproduced in this book.
Any omissions will be rectified in subse-
quent printings if notice is given
to the publisher.

# Contents

CHAPTER 1

A Day in the Life . . . . .4

CHAPTER 2

Food to Eat and
a Place to Live . . . . . .10

CHAPTER 3

Family Life . . . . . . . .21

CHAPTER 4

Predators and
Other Threats. . . . . .26

Other Resources. . . . . . . . . . . .30

# A Day in the Life

It's late in the afternoon. A female rabbit hops into a field and starts to **graze**. It eats, looks up for danger, and then eats some more.

After grazing awhile, the rabbit stops to sniff. Clover! It hops over and nibbles. Then it hears a noise. Not stopping to check it out, it hops under a bush.

RABBIT FEATURES

LONG EARS

NOSE

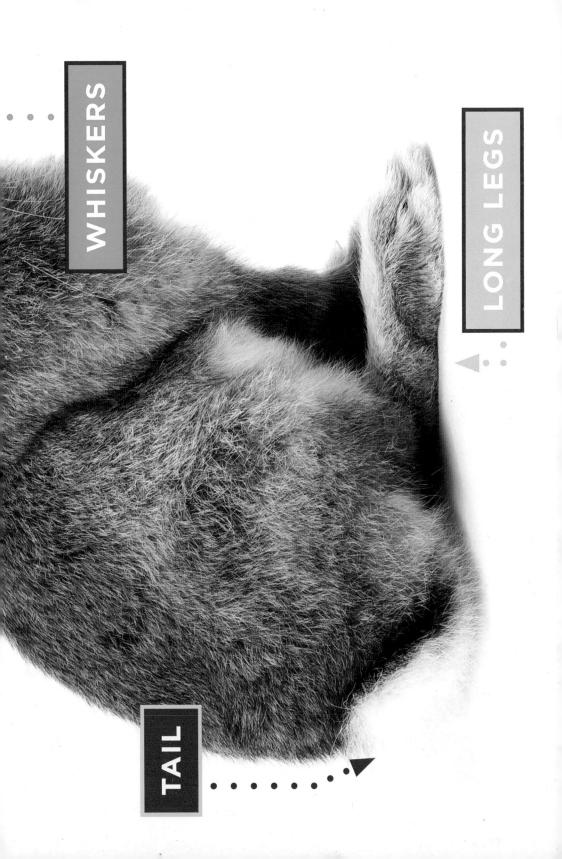

WHISKERS

LONG LEGS

TAIL

INCHES 0    2

**COMPARING RABBITS' SIZES**

**Pygmy Rabbit**
9.4 TO 11.6 INCHES
(24 to 29 centimeters)
0.6 TO 1.0 POUNDS
(.3 to .5 kilograms)

**Swamp Rabbit**
16 TO 22 INCHES
(41 to 56 cm)
4 TO 6 POUNDS
(1.8 to 2.7 kg)

POUNDS 0    1

# Babies in the Burrow

The rabbit returns to the **burrow** where its babies wait. It feeds them and then leaves. It will be back the next night to feed them again.

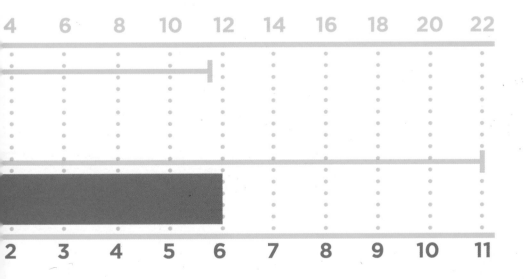

# CHAPTER 2

# Food to Eat

## and a Place to Live

Rabbits are **herbivores**, which means they only eat plants. To find enough food, they eat a wide range of plants. In summer, they eat grass, flowers, and clover. In winter, they eat twigs and bark.

## Super Sight

A rabbit can see very well. Its eyes are placed on the sides of its head. With them, it can see all around itself.

## Supper Time

Rabbits go out to eat at sunrise and early evening. Some eat at night too. As they eat, they sniff all the time. They sniff to smell **predators**. They don't want to become a meal for some other animal.

A rabbit needs to eat its food twice. First, it eats a plant. Then it pushes the food out its backside as soft balls. It then eats the balls.

# By the Numbers

**28**

TEETH

**1 to 2 YEARS**

AVERAGE LIFE SPAN

**18**
MILES
(29 KILOMETERS)
PER HOUR

AVERAGE RUNNING SPEED

ABOUT **1**
OUNCE
(28 GRAMS)

WEIGHT OF
EASTERN
COTTONTAILS
AT BIRTH

**ABOUT 28**
SPECIES OF RABBITS

**12**
LARGEST
LITTER
SIZE

LONGEST
**EARS**
**31.1**
INCHES
(79 CM)

# Home Sweet Home

Rabbits live in most parts of the world. They live in woods, fields, deserts, and swamps. Most rabbits live alone. But some live in large groups.

Wherever they live, rabbits need a place to rest. This place must hide them well. It must also keep them cool. Some rabbits rest under bushes. Some rest in burrows.

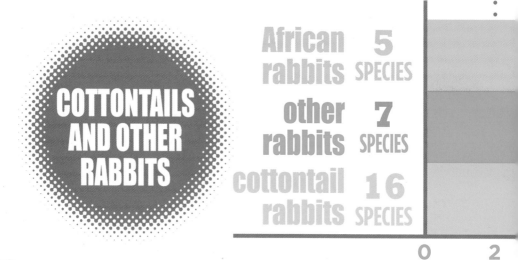

COTTONTAILS AND OTHER RABBITS

African rabbits 5 SPECIES

other rabbits 7 SPECIES

cottontail rabbits 16 SPECIES

0     2

There are many types of rabbits. **The cottontails** are the largest group.

4  6  8  10  12  14  16

## Rabbit Range Map

# CHAPTER 3

# Family Life

A female rabbit is called a doe. Most does have more than one **litter** each year. Litters are not all the same size. Most have at least two babies. The babies are called kittens. Some litters have up to eight kittens.

## Rabbit Nests

When it's time to give birth, a doe makes a nest. It might dig a small bowl in the ground. Or it will dig a burrow. The doe lines its nest with grass. It adds fur it has plucked from its belly.

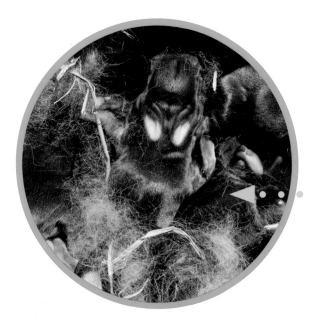

# Rabbit Nest Features

KITTENS PILED TOGETHER TO KEEP WARM

WELL HIDDEN FROM PREDATORS

FUR FROM A DOE

## Kittens

Kittens are born with closed eyes. They have no hair. They drink milk from their mothers for three to four weeks. Then they start to eat plants.

Once their kittens are born, does leave their nests. They only go back to feed the babies.

# CHAPTER 4

# Predators
## and Other Threats

Rabbits have many predators. Bobcats, wolves, snakes, and birds all eat rabbits. When a rabbit smells a predator, it freezes. Without movement, predators might not see the rabbit.

# Rabbit Ecosystem

Some people think of rabbits as pests. Rabbits eat garden plants and farmers' crops. But rabbits do good things too. They provide food for predators. Their burrows are used by other small animals. Rabbits are important parts of their **ecosystems**.

This **food chain** shows what rabbits eat. It also shows what eats rabbits.

**WOLVES**  **OWLS**  **SNAKES**

**RABBITS**

**GRASS, FLOWERS, AND CLOVER**  **TWIGS AND BARK**

**burrow** (BUR-oh)—a hole in the ground made by an animal for shelter or protection

**ecosystem** (E-co-sys-tum)—a community of living things in one place

**food chain** (FOOD CHAYN)—a series of plants and animals in which each uses the next in the series as a food source

**graze** (GRAYZ)—to feed on growing grass or herbs

**herbivore** (HERB-uh-vor)—a plant-eating animal

**litter** (LITER)—the young born to an animal at a single time

**predator** (PRED-uh-tuhr)—an animal that eats other animals

## BOOKS

**Graubart, Norman D.** *How to Track a Rabbit.* Scatalog: A Kid's Field Guide to Animal Poop. New York: Windmill, 2015.

**Heos, Bridget**. *Do You Really Want a Rabbit?* Do You Really Want …? Mankato, MN: Amicus, 2014.

**Newman, Aline Alexander**. *Rascally Rabbits! And More True Stories of Animals Behaving Badly.* NGK Chapters. Washington, D.C.: National Geographic Children's Books, 2016.

## WEBSITES

Cottontail Rabbit
**animals.nationalgeographic.com/animals/ mammals/cottontail-rabbit/**

Eastern Cottontail
**www.biokids.umich.edu/critters/Sylvilagus_ floridanus/**

Rabbit
**www.bbc.co.uk/nature/life/European_Rabbit**

# INDEX

## F

features, 6–7, 11, 14–15

food, 4, 10, 13, 24, 28–29

## H

habitats, 16

## K

kittens, 9, 15, 21, 23, 24

## L

litters, 15, 21

## N

nests, 9, 22–23, 24

## P

predators, 13, 23, 26, 28–29

## R

ranges, 16, 18–19

## S

sizes, 8–9, 15

speeds, 14